PTSD

TO

Freedom

No More War Within

LINDA DIANE WATTLEY
WILLIAM SUMNER

Cover Designer

Creative Ankh Designs

Copyright 2018 by Linda Diane Wattley
& William Sumner
All Rights Reserved

Wattley, Linda Diane / Sumner, William
ISBN:
"PTSD to Freedom: *No More War Within*" /
Linda Diane Wattley & William Sumner – 1st ed.

No part of this publication may be reproduced, except in the case of quotation for articles, reviews, or stored in any retrieval system, or transmitted in any form or by any means, electronic, mechanical, recording, photo-copying or otherwise, without written permission from the publisher. For information regarding permission, contact: Linda Diane Wattley

Printed in the USA

PTSD TO FREEDOM
No More War Within

TABLE OF CONTENTS

- ... 1 ... INTRODUCTION: Why This Book Was Written
- ... 3 ... CHAPTER 1: Undiagnosed Childhood PTSD
- ... 7 ... CHAPTER 2: Flashbacks/ Domestic Violence
- ... 9 ... CHAPTER 3: My Fault/ Attempted Rape
- ... 11 ... CHAPTER 4: Just When I Thought It Was Safe: Divorce/Alcoholism
- ... 15 ... CHAPTER 5: Not Now: Sudden Death
- ... 19 ... CHAPTER 6: Why Adults Are Not Happy: Broken Heart/ Instant Widow
- ... 25 ... CHAPTER 7: Giving Up: Car Crash/Body Trauma
- ... 31 ... CHAPTER 8: PTSD and Me: Diagnosis

PART II: LIVING WITH PTSD

... 41 ... CHAPTER 9: Family with PTSD

... 49 ... CHAPTER 10: Daily Struggles with PTSD

... 57 ... CHAPTER 11: The Truth Will Set You Free: The Catalyst of PTSD

PART III: THE GIFT OF FREEDOM

... 75 ... CHAPTER 12: First Step to Freedom: Be Willing to Learn

... 79 ... CHAPTER 13: Trust in PTSD to PTSG: Introduction

... 83 ... CHAPTER 14: Preparation for Removing the PTSD Label

... 93 ... CHAPTER 15: The Brain is the Hard Drive for the Mind

... 97 ... CHAPTER 16: Stress Perspectives

... 101 ... CHAPTER 17: The Impact of Labelling

... 105 ... CHAPTER 18: Goodbye PTSD Label

... 115 ... CONCLUSION

... 127 ... ABOUT THE AUTHORS

DEDICATION

As we face the world today, we cannot ignore the human struggle to survive traumatic experiences to the heart, mind, body, and soul.

We have been shocked and thrown into unwanted life-changing experiences, but we keep breathing.

We are breathing because we are alive and must continue to move forward no matter what. In some cases, our wounds are visible and other cases the wounds are unseen getting no empathy from anyone.

We face the world as though we are not suffering because we must, it is not an option.

We smile, laugh and meet our daily requirements in hopes that one day when we wake up we will discover our suffering was only a dream.

"**PTSD TO FREEDOM:** *No More War Within*" is dedicated to us, the ones who will wake up from this nightmare.

REVIEWS
for PTSD to Freedom

All of us are going through challenges in life, and for some it might feel as though you're on a battlefield every day that you open your eyes and try to make it through the day. Fortunately for us, we have examples of individuals who have been able to not just recognize areas of trauma in their lives but take steps to alleviate that. Linda Diane Wattley and William Sumner are such examples, and their book, "**PTSD TO FREEDOM**", allows you to know how you can do the same.

This is a journey that will take time, effort and most importantly honesty with yourself, but the end result is one that will give you peace and allow you to realize that a more fulfilling life is possible for you. Don't allow what has occurred in your life and around you to keep you a prisoner of war. Avail yourself of the help "**PTSD TO FREEDOM**" offers and look ahead towards the future with hope.

~ Cyrus Webb, Media Personality/Top Amazon Reviewer

In 1999 I met a man and fell in love with him. To tell you a little about him, his Dad died when he was 2, he grew up with a single mother and a brother that was 10 years older. Most of his time was spent on his own, taking care of himself, a very sad childhood. A few years after high school he was drafted for the Vietnam War. After his discharge he came home and went to work as a Firefighter which he retired from in 1999. During this time, he also took care of his mother until she died in the year 2000. After her death I let him move in with me. From the beginning of our relationship I noticed that he drank heavily but not every day. The nights he didn't drink he would wake up yelling from bad dreams. This caused his drinking to increase and after almost 19 years, he drinks EVERY night, or I should say evening since he starts at 3:00 P.M. and is pretty wasted by 6:00 P.M. after consuming at least a 5th of liquor. His moods changed. He would become angry over nothing and started talking about being old and ready to die. This man just turned 69 years old, which isn't old anymore.

Until recently, I had never heard of PTSD and didn't really know what it was. After reading **"PTSD to Freedom: *No More War Within"*,** I learned a lot and know what to watch for. In the beginning I thought it was simply because of his time in Vietnam. I've come to learn that it does come from Vietnam but is also comes from the loss of his Dad, the loss of his Mother and his years as a firefighter. When you combine all of this, he has it bad.

So, if you have a loved one who has had any type of trauma in their life, please read this book so it can open your eyes too. Reading it won't allow you to cure them but it will help you understand what they are going through – past, present and future.

~ Martha A Cheves, Author
Lives with someone with PTSD

~~~~~~~~~~~

The authors are Veterans of the United States Army and are very familiar with PTSD. Linda Diane Wattley starts the book with her life and experiences which were causal to her diagnosis of PTSD. Eventually she sought out a psychologist and during that visit she decided that she was not prepared to be guided by anyone and had to figure this out for herself and began to research PTSD.

In the next pages she introduces PTSG. Post-Traumatic Stress Growth which she describes as the key what will help enlighten us as to the degree of infiltration of shock by traumatic experiences and how we can lessen their degree.

She also takes the time to thank Davon J. Morris author of "Evil Hours: Biography of PTSD" as his book provided her with the major tools she was missing to better live with PTSD.

Further along, she introduces you to the author William Sumner, who re-introduces tools we already use but do not maximize. Sumner is the creator of a coaching system that gets you from PTSD to PTSG which is a tools-based system. It is further described in the book and at the end of the book. There is also a link available to find out more about it. Sumner also references NLP (Neuro-Linguistic Programming), which he says is "massively effective."

I'd like to try to explain this in layman's terms since I've read the book three times. If you have a trigger and replace the horrific thought that makes you react badly with a better, nicer thought then when that trigger happens, and you think the better, nicer thought your reaction to the trigger will be a more pleasant one and not a "stress" triggering one hence less trauma, less stress. Sumner provides a couple of examples of this in the book and I think that is why it is so understandable for me to be able to put this amazing tool into layman's terms myself.

This book, PTSG, NLP, etc. are all part of the journey on the road to removing the PTSD label. He also goes on to talk about toxic stress and the impact of labelling.

As a sufferer of PTSD, myself I found this book to be very helpful in understanding where the label fits in. How interesting it is that one can change one's own thinking, maybe not easily at first, to help one's self to maintain less stress and less reactive moments regarding trauma. After reading this I found myself catching myself reacting badly to certain situations and pulling my reactions back and redirecting my thoughts to better react and not feel so badly about reacting because it was a better choice.

I would suggest that if upon reading this it helps you in the least bit rethink or adjust your thinking about PTSD and reactions that maybe you should investigate the coaching system and/or talking to these authors or checking out the radio shows or speaking engagements they are involved in. They certainly have good, positive, and interesting things to say and their knowledge is definitely something to listen to and entertain.

~ Anastasia Young, Editor/Proofreader, Chauncey's Premier Editing. She has PTSD and can relate to others who suffer with it.

INTRODUCTION
WHY THIS BOOK WAS WRITTEN

After I wrote my first book pertaining to PTSD, Post-Traumatic Stress Disorder, "**Soldier with a Backpack: *Living and Dying Simultaneously*,**" I learned a lot more about the experience from my readers and interviewers.

The knowledge and wisdom were so freeing and encouraging that it gave me the desire to share it with the world.

One of the most profound and life-changing nuggets of truth and wisdom came from William Sumner, the creator of "The Inevitable You" ®, a Coaching System designed to help people grow, change, transform and heal their lives in ways they never could imagine.

What we have to share in "**PTSD TO FREEDOM:** *No More War Within*" promises to present tools of pure transformation for anyone choosing to live their best self at all times. It is with great honor and love that this book is written. Your freedom is our freedom.

CHAPTER 1
UNDIAGNOSED CHILDHOOD PTSD

Ever since I can remember, as a child I had this silent need to understand why people were so unhappy and unable to love one another. It seemed adults were always fretful and disappointed with life's experiences. Then it happened, I became an adult and soon learned there was nothing easy about life's journey for anyone especially innocent children.

I will never forget the day when I realized prior to becoming an adult, my childhood traumatic experiences had already tainted my chances of becoming a happy adult.

Marcus, my youngest son, and I were having dinner one evening and he shared a conversation he and his wife were having about their childhood. Feeling relaxed and anxious to hear what he had to say, I sat quietly waiting to hear his story.

"Katie and I were discussing our childhood. We asked each other, What was the first memory you have of being a child?"

I told her my memory was when I was about four years-old. "I had gone to see my mom, and when I got to the doorway of her bedroom, she was in her bed crying. I turned and walked away."

Marcus continued sharing their conversation with me and what Katie, his wife shared was a very pleasant memory. I was glad to hear that because it gave me a chance to attempt to take in his first childhood memory especially when he told me he later learned crying meant the person was unhappy.

He said all this with a perplexed look on his face as though he was reliving the moment.

"What was your first memory as a child, Mom?" Marcus asked.

Being stung by this new information pertaining to my life and my son's memory, a serious wave of emotions rushed through my body feeling like a pressure cooker about to blow a gasket.

Immediately, an attempt was made to eliminate the growing pressure of piercing energy rushing through my body. Appearance-wise, I was very successful in containing the pressure; but my insides collapsed feeling every bit like being burned.

"Wow! That was a tear jerker, Marcus." I said as I fought back the unwanted tears.

He smiled and still waited for me to answer.

"You really don't want to know," I said with a painful look on my face.

"Your dad?"

Sitting there feeling the aftermath of the threatening pressure now shooting through my nervous system, I couldn't help but wonder what it was making me feel like I was about to blow a gasket. It was as if whatever it was had been waiting for a golden opportunity to attack me, break me down and change my life forever. For a minute there I thought I was having a nervous breakdown. If it wasn't a demon attempting to destroy me, what was it?

This is just one of the questions I asked myself. Where and what do I have stored in my inner parts from my past? How do I dispose of its impact on my present moments? Where do I begin?

CHAPTER 2
FLASHBACKS/ DOMESTIC VIOLENCE

After that dinner with Marcus, I was reminded of major scenes in my life besides being molested by my father at the age of three. The vibrations of fear echoed through my being as I vividly remember one night during a rainstorm my father beating my mother so viciously as though she was not his wife and the mother of his children. Instead, he attacked her as if she was a prowler threating his family.

My brothers and I looked on through the big picture window in the front room of our house. Through the thunder and lightning, we heard our mother crying and begging him to stop body slamming her to the ground and punching her like she was a punching bag. It was a terrible sight to see and hear. She was drenched in mud by the time he finished with her leaving her to fend for herself as she struggled to stand up only to fall back down again. He just stepped over her and came in the house and sent us to bed.

This was the first time we saw him beat her up outside the home. Usually we would hear my father throwing her up against walls and calling her horrible names while she screamed and cried for him to stop.

CHAPTER 3
MY FAULT/ATTEMPTED RAPE

For quite some time, I was out of touch with the reality of losing my virginity to my father and when I finally remembered, it was a nightmare. Along with that, I still have flashbacks of the night my father's life changed forever.

"Stop! Don't touch me! Leave me alone!" I yelled as my father attempted to corner me off alone in our basement. He wanted to fondle me, touch my body in a way a boyfriend would touch a teenaged girl. I was crying and shaking so much, he stopped trying to undress me.

To this day, I still have flashbacks of clinging to the zipper of my jeans that prevented him from pulling my pants down.

"I am so sorry, Lyn, I will never touch you again. I promise," He said while backing away from me. There was such an apologetic and saddened look changing his demeanor, I felt guilty for not allowing him to touch me. It was not normal for me to disappoint him which caused me to feel horribly bad inside.

Before that night was over, my father secured that promise in a way that never entered his mind. He was shot and paralyzed from the waist down. He and my stepmother got in a heated argument resulting in him getting shot in the back by her as he was walking down the steps to go to work.

My brothers had no idea of the guilty feelings racing through my mind. This is my fault; I should have never caused him to promise to not touch me again. All night my heart was aching, and I just couldn't stop crying, tossing and turning trying so hard to understand why I didn't let him touch me. Things would be so different if I had.

CHAPTER 4
JUST WHEN I THOUGHT IT WAS SAFE: DIVORCE/ALCHOLISM

My parents were eventually divorced. Because my father had more money to pay attorney fees, he won custody of me and my brothers. We lived with him and our new stepmother and stepsiblings. When my brothers and I reached the age where we could choose which parent we preferred to live with, we chose to return to our mother.

I was so anxious to live with my mom once again. My moment of potential bliss was snatched away the moment I took a blow to the face causing me to receive a black eye for the first time in my life.

I will never forget that night. It was a horrible experience.

"You winch! You love that woman!"

"Let go of me!" I yelled.

Suddenly, I felt a hard blow to my left eye. A sharp pain shot through it making me feel dizzy. She kept tugging and punching on me. The buttons on my blouse popped off from the strong yanking and pulling to mobilize me so I couldn't move. Eventually I pushed her away from me and ran out the front door in the middle of the night.

Outside, huffing and puffing I struggled to catch my breath. Because my eye was beginning to swell, reality kicked in: my mother attacked me like she hated me. All this animosity was because I loved my stepmother, a woman who allowed me to call her mom, a woman who clothed, fed me and combed my hair. What was I supposed to do? I needed a mom.

I had to find a safe place to stay for the night. Going back to my father was out of the question. I knew my mother was intoxicated and would be back to herself once she slept it off, so I pulled my blouse together and ran across the street to my friend Henrietta's house.

When she and her mom opened the door, their faces scared the hell out of me. I must have looked bad. They thought someone had tried to rape or kill me. Embarrassed, I had to tell them my mom had been drinking and went on a rampage and it was focused on me.

By the time my brothers and I made our way back to mom, she was a battered woman whose abusive husband had stolen her children from her and took up with another woman who had a child by him. Heavy drinking became a way to kill the pain. She was the first and only person to beat me up and give me a black eye. When mom was not intoxicated, we all got along fine.

To this day there are times when I am enjoying my mother and she is having several drinks causing the mother I encountered as a child to surface; a trigger goes off and instantly I am very unhappy and defensive, and she has no idea why I am not the same person I was before she became intoxicated. All I can do is wait until my wonderful mother comes back before I am comfortable again with her.

I still remember the red cotton blouse with white buttons being literally shredded by the anger and hands of my mother.

CHAPTER 5
NOT NOW: SUDDEN DEATH

My big brother Anthony was a miracle child born with a heart defect...doctors did not expect him to live beyond ten years old. Miraculously, he lived to be nineteen years old. Sirens of emergency vehicles to this day reminds me of the heart-wrenching and rough ride I took in the ambulance that carried him to Akron Children's Hospital.

One night, Anthony and I talked about our dreams and goals until the wee hours of the morning. He wanted to play football so badly knowing he had a heart condition. I asked him to promise me before he started preparing for football to first have a physical to make sure his heart was strong enough. You couldn't tell him he hadn't grown out of his heart defect because he had already proven the doctors wrong about how much time he had to live. He told me we'll see and we both fell asleep.

Startled out of my sleep a few hours later by the urgent, harsh and loud banging on the door, I stumbled to the front door to see who was there. It was one of our neighbors who knew us well.

"Anthony fell out on the track!"

"Anthony?"

I ran and looked in his room and sure enough, my big brother was not there. This had to be a dream. Just a few hours ago, we were talking, laughing and encouraging each other about our future. It was my mom's birthday. This could not be happening. Wait a minute, he just fell out! I must go help him!

With no shoes on, half clothes and pajamas on, I ran barefooted down the street to the Wooster Branch Library where I found Anthony lying flat on his back, motionless. He was all alone.

His body was wrapped in a black garbage bag with his shirt and pants covering the bag. Wearing a plastic bag was a new way of making you sweat while trying to lose weight. His glasses lay crushed and bent out of shape because of his body dropping to the ground.

It was over an hour with no signs of an ambulance to take him to Akron Children's Hospital where my mother worked. As I sat down beside him lying on the ground, I considered his eyes because they were wide open. There was no personality or any signs of a cry for help. In fact, his eyes looked like marbles. Gently, I closed them and waited for the ambulance. I no longer had a big brother.

To this day, I remember what Anthony was wearing on July 30, 1973: a brown shirt, a black plastic trash bag, a white T shirt and tan, blue and brown striped pants and his gold wire-framed glasses.

Anthony was not the only one I loved who suddenly died in less than a month, my friend Paul, was working on a car in his driveway. While under the car, it slipped off the jack and crushed him to death. He was my walk-to-school buddy. In fact, we walked the same path to school my brother's body was found on.

In my junior year I walked to school alone.

What do I think about now? Is this what we are living for? To die? No one is asking me if I am alright.

CHAPTER 6
WHY ADULTS ARE NOT HAPPY: BROKEN HEART/INSTANT WIDOW

Two years after Anthony died, I graduated and joined the United States Army.

It was during my time in the Army I finally began to feel there was hope for me to live a happy and healthy life. During this time, I met the love of my life, Robert D. Wattley, Jr. We clicked instantly. He was my best friend and a person who loved everything about me even though I did not understand why. I called him Bob.

When we completed our term in the service, we were married and had two wonderful sons, Robert, III and Marcus. We loved our life and enjoyed our children. My husband was a proud father who spent a lot of time with his sons even though they were very young, Robert III was four and Marcus was two and a half when our lives changed forever.

One September evening, the leaves had fallen to the ground, the sun was shining ever so brightly because it was nearing sunset. He and I made plans to take the boys for ice cream cones when he returned home from work. I ran errands until it was time for him to come home. One of the stops I made was by my mother's house, and as soon as I pulled up in the driveway, the telephone rang. My mom came to the door and told me Bob was on the phone. This was surprising since I didn't tell him I was going to my mother's house, so I was eager to see what prompted the call.

"Hey!"

"Hi Baby, I just called to tell you I am so proud of the mother you are to our children and I love you."

"I love you, too…guess what? I made the Dean's list!"

"Of course, you did, Baby; you are the best."

"Bob, do you want me to pick you up? I've done all my running."

"No, I will meet you at the house."

The boys and I went to the house to wait for him. We were ready to go for a ride and eat some ice cream when suddenly, I heard a strong and immediate knock on my front door. I told my sons to sit down on the couch while I answered the door.

"Mrs. Wattley?"

"Yes?" I answered quickly as I tried to understand why a police officer was standing at my front door.

"My name is Sheriff Winston... I am sorry to say this, but your husband was involved in a serious vehicular accident. He has been transported to Akron City Hospital. You must go there as soon as possible. I'm just so sorry, Ma'am."

I backed up from the door, looked at our children. Paralyzed and speechless, I just stood there for a minute. This just could not be happening. My neighbor's husband, Mr. Bass, drove me to the hospital while my neighbor, Mary Jo, tended to our children.

As I began the long walk to the emergency room entrance of the hospital,

I looked up to the sky and asked God, "Please do not take my husband." Immediately I heard it as plain as day, *pray for something else, I already have.*

I walked into the emergency room area, identified myself and asked to see my husband. I was told to be seated in an isolated room alone and someone would come for me when they are ready for me to see him.

Nearing an hour, I paced and began to demand to see him. The doctor told me he didn't think it was a good idea. I got a little hysterical in my actions and voice and again, I demanded that they "Let me see him right now!" Then the strangest thing happened…I felt my husband vibrate a message to me to not come into the room. At this point I stopped shouting and jerked away from security. I pulled myself together and walked out of the hospital. I could hear a message over the intercom warning people that a deranged woman was in the area.

Once outside the hospital, my mother walked towards the emergency room entrance. She tried to communicate with me to find out what was going on, but I just told her that Bob was gone, and I just kept walking.

Now I understand why adults are not happy, their hearts get broken and their hopes and dreams get stolen.

CHAPTER 7
GIVING UP: CAR CRASH/ BODY TRAUMA

I now must face life without my husband and the father of our sons. Who would have told me I would become a widow at the age of twenty-eight years old? The comprehension of it consumed me daily. When I was not tending to my children, I was captured in the reality of being a widow.

When you have such a tragic experience as this, the sudden death of your spouse due to an irresponsible driver driving her brown Corvette over 100 miles an hour in a residential area it blows your mind. Where are you and your loved ones safe? My husband was just a passenger involved in a fatal car accident involving four people who all walked away but him.

I remember sitting there looking at my sons not sure if they understood what happened to their father. The last time they saw him, he was in a casket. For sure, I knew Marcus was too young to understand. Robert, III, it was a different story, I saw it in his eyes, he was broken. He knew the next week after his father's death, the birthday they always shared together could not and would not be happening ever again. At the age of five, he learned like adults, life is very difficult to live.

I pained at the reality I could not remove Robert's pain and Marcus would not have a memory of his own, ever, of his dad. It was then I understood why some people contemplate suicide not just for themselves but for their loved ones as well. Why face another day not knowing if it was time for another one of us to die?

All I would have to do is prepare for bed and turn on the gas on the stove and never wake up; all three of us would be with Bob forever. Why didn't I do it? Because that same voice that told me to pray for something else when I asked God to not take my husband would not let me.

Realizing God had us, I proceeded to be the best mother I could possibly be to my children. I equipped them with love, guidance, spiritual truths and tools that would prepare them to have an amazing adult life just in case my life ended abruptly as did their father's. Would you not believe I was almost killed in a car accident two years later after my husband's car accident?

The memory is vivid. It was one of those perfect summer days where the morning sun was gracing the earth like it was heaven. I was feeling so blessed and thankful for my life as I had come to accept my plight. I was on my way to work as the church secretary of True Love Baptist Church in Fort Wayne, Indiana. Feeling so good, I left for work early and was taking my time getting there. I stopped at a red light and didn't understand why my car was still moving through the intersection. With my foot still on the brake, my car continued coasting through the intersection forcing me to steer out of traffic to land on the sidewalk nearest the street.

I climbed out of my 1976 engine red Nova to learn the back end of my car was crushed all the way into my back window. A truck driver had jumped out his truck and asked me if I was alright. He let me know he had called the police and an ambulance and he was so sorry for hitting my car. Then he told me something I will never forget.

"I couldn't stop, all I could do was steer my truck away from your gas tank because I knew if I hit it, your car would have blown up! I am so sorry!"

He could not stop because he had 50 tons of asphalt loaded on the back of his truck even on his brakes, he couldn't stop. This accident put me in the hospital for three months because they could not figure out why I continued to have blackouts and speech impairment. In the meantime, my sons struggled to be happy without their mom. Eventually I was diagnosed with a severe whiplash, concussion and trauma to my body. All of this effected my memory, thought processing, speech, walking, shoulder blade pain, spasms, standing ability and mood. I was thrown into deep depression. I was told I would be on muscle relaxers for the rest of my life.

Against medical advice, I checked myself out of the hospital to get my children so that they would know they did not lose another parent.

The road back was a nightmare. Muscle relaxers were turning me into a marshmallow. For my children, I put the muscle relaxers down and faced the daily crises my body was enduring. I was convinced I would not live to see my children become adults because so much trauma was visiting my body. And, according to my life experiences, we do not have long to live anyway.

CHAPTER 8
PTSD AND ME: DIAGNOSIS

Eventually I began to realize I was concerned about what would be considered a normal state of mind. I was confident in my role as a mother because I knew I loved my children and always based my decisions on their well-being but the moment I had time for myself, I was in a very dark place. My mind kept returning to painful memories from my childhood right up to the voice of the truck driver that was the catalyst of changing my life forever and sparing it as well.

I didn't believe in psychologists, but I knew I had to try to save myself, so I could continue to be there for my children, so I scheduled an appointment and visited a psychologist who was more of the new age way of thinking which made it seem more spiritual than psychological. She informed me immediately that I was suffering with PTSD, Post-Traumatic Stress Disorder.

I stood up once she explained to me that how I am reacting to life is very normal due to my history of trauma. I exhaled because she said I was having a normal reaction to life. She let me know each case of PTSD is unique and treatment varies from medications to meditations and psychological experiments of revisiting each trigger of memories that caused grief.

Though she was kind and I loved her approach, I was not prepared to be guided by anyone. I had to figure this thing out for myself. I began to research PTSD and I got a better understanding of just what trauma meant for me and my life's journey. It was fascinating to realize that the answers are there if you seek them out.

Out of trauma, much drama occurs. Trauma has so many levels of appearing in our lives from the war zones where our soldiers witness death and the survival of death, vehicular accidents, murders, natural disasters, divorce, illnesses, rape, domestic violence, sudden deaths of our loved ones; the list is unending.

Directly and indirectly these endless forms of trauma infiltrate our lives. These experiences are so extremely personal and painful, we feel inhuman and embarrassed because we have an unnerving feeling of being naked when it occurs. It is a type of nakedness uncommon to the human eye because trauma vibrates heavily on the inside rocking every logical reality to nothingness. The sudden impact of trauma is like a glitch of nature being surreal. It is the big secret we as individuals and as a collective people keep hidden in our hearts.

The aftermath of trauma cannot be hidden. It permeates through our being during our waking and sleeping states of being. Something about trauma immediately makes us think no one will get it and there is no need in seeking outside of ourselves for someone to understand and comfort us because to convey our suffering seems impossible to describe. This causes the alienation process to begin.

How can anyone relate to us when he or she did not experience the inner catastrophic attack in our mind and nervous system? In fact, it is still there lurking around inside our bodies; a private hell we want to destroy. Sometimes the feelings and fearful thoughts of the new sudden experience feels like an avalanche erupted in the core of our being. The normal rationalizing of connecting thoughts and feelings begin to feel like an inner turmoil as the thoughts and emotions are slipping and sliding in their attempts to connect. Not able to get a grip on it at times can make us feel like killing the body to stop the madness.

In days to come, we use every ounce of our energy and mental ability to present ourselves to the world that all is well, so please stop looking at me. Often it is when we get into our vehicles alone and lock ourselves in that some of the aftermath of the trauma seeps out causing us to release tears and anguish. By the time we reach our destination, we are once again able to produce a person free of pain.

At times, we do have a euphoric moment realizing we didn't let the private torture kill us and we're still standing. The cycles begin all over again, sometimes in lesser or greater degrees. This continued cycle creates an epidemic of victims becoming consciously and or subconsciously unable to love or accept love. They would rather face life without a heart because it is much easier than to run the risk of becoming brokenhearted again.

Cycles can be broken when light is shone on reality. This is my purpose to shine light on the personal aftermath of trauma and to consider the possibility you and someone you love just might be undiagnosed or diagnosed with PTSD, Post-Traumatic Stress Disorder.

PART II:

LIVING WITH PTSD

*"If an egg is broken by outside force,
Life ends.
If broken by inside force,
Life begins.
Great things always begin from inside."*
~ Jim Kwik

"Hello, my name is Linda Diane Wattley, I have PTSD."

"Welcome Linda, glad to have you join us tonight."

I imagine this is how it would be if I joined a support group for Post-Traumatic Stress Disorder. This part of the book is to reveal the truth about PTSD. When you reach the end of this book, you will discover the PTSD label is no longer necessary to identify yourself.

PTSD is a unique, powerful and universal reaction to life. It is not just happening to our soldiers returning from war. Post-Traumatic Stress Disorder happens to anyone who has been shocked by the traumatic experiences of life. The question is what degree of it has been infiltrated and how do we lessen this degree. In the pages to follow, we will learn how to be more than the diagnosis of PTSD. In the end, we will be enlightened by PTSG, Post-Traumatic Stress Growth.

CHAPTER 9
FAMILY WITH PTSD

The human being is a fragile flower.
Any stone can crush you.
Any accident and you are gone...
  ~ Osho

I know without a doubt that there is a God because based on my early beginnings in life, I was not equipped to be a great parent or person. So, what I lacked, God provided, and I am very aware of the many gifts of love he fed my soul.

Once I was diagnosed with Post-Traumatic Stress Disorder, I kept it to myself. I never told anyone about it. I learned how to live with it one day at a time with trial and error. Mental illness was not a popular subject during the time of my diagnosis as it is today. Not that I was ashamed, I just didn't see any reason to share it. Eventually I learned it is not actually a mental illness as much of it being a psychological injury which made me feel more comfortable with my apparent issue. It wasn't until my son was diagnosed with PTSD that it was no longer a solo and private experience.

Before I go any farther, I must thank Davon J. Morris, author of "Evil Hours: Biography of PTSD" and his 50 backers who pledged to make sure his story was told. His book provided me the tools I was missing to better live with PTSD.

I must acknowledge every veteran who experienced the traumas of war. Thank you for not giving up and for constantly seeking support to be a better presence in this world. Not only do I want to acknowledge our soldiers, but every person who puts their life on the line be it fireman, police officer, nurse, doctor, paramedics, anyone whose job is to protect and assist in the continuation of human life, thank you. I pray for you to not be destroyed in your efforts to serve mankind.

My son served two terms in Iraq, his unit, the 1484th Transportation Company of Akron, Ohio, was one of the first to enter Fallujah in 2005. He returned to Iraq with another unit, the 1483rd

Transportation Company of Toledo, Ohio, in 2008 where he served more than a year. It was not until 2014 when he was officially diagnosed with PTSD. It was his last serious episode with PTSD that sped up my needed attention on the veracity of the severity of this disorder.

Because of Davon Morris, my research was made fruitful. In one book, I gained much understanding of the powerful impact it has on our soldiers' lives and how the world views and handles the disorder. I also became more conscious of how awesomely resilient Robert is. He was still in soldier-mode quietly battling this disorder, yet able to love and provide for his family as though all was well. We knew he was having some difficulties adapting to civilian life during his first return from Iraq, but this was to be expected. But there were times his patience was short in his interactions with people. His sleep patterns were constantly disturbed with nightmares from war, and there were times he had difficulty focusing on what he was currently doing.

For him, life was simpler in Iraq because he knew exactly what he had to do, when to do it, and how. He had no problem risking his life to protect his comrades.

He remained in the United States National Guard and continued to meet the requirements of duty dismissing him from his work obligations once a month and a two-week regimen once a year. He always has plans and goals and is always able to complete and reach them.

Everything appeared to be normal.

He was working, spending quality time with his family and friends but it always seemed like something was irritating him. Sometimes his patience was so short, he appeared angry towards you. It began to be obvious to me that one contributing factor to his growing mood swings was the presence of fatigue. When he was fatigued, he ran the risk of a potential meltdown.

The thing about reaching this level was it wouldn't dawn on him he was exhausted, like he didn't see it coming. He worked and supported others in a high capacity coupled with sleep deprivation, but there just never seemed to be signs telling him to slow down, as if he was invincible. When I would suggest he slowed down, he'd avoid me. But once the mental and emotional collapse began to take place, Robert would fight for his life. His fighting for his life holds me in great esteem for the person he is. I appreciate the fact he reaches out while seeing his life being pulled down by the pits of hell. Each time he has an episode, I would ask him what triggered it. His reply always was, "I keep telling you I have PTSD." I'd share the experience with his brother, Marcus, and he'd ask me the same question: "What triggered it?"

Because we are so closely knitted in standing watch for each other, we realize our patterns and routines. Marcus and I felt something, or somebody triggered the onset because we have followed him through each episode and noticed something happened or someone pushed him to the edge expecting too much support from him in making their lives easier. Though we saw this happening, we did not connect it to PTSD. To us, it was simple exhaustive stress.

One episode took place allowing me to connect more to the experience because he called me and began to share what he was experiencing. His special emphasis was on being tired of holding back the daily struggle of the PTSD constantly trying to take over his life. All this time I thought his exhaustion was his life activities, but he let me know it was the battling of the nightmares, the daily constant watch of making the best decisions and putting forth effort to be comfortable in his environment. This made him feel like he no longer wanted to be here. When I asked him, "What about Jaelynn?" who is his only child, his quick reply was, "You don't get it. This has nothing to do with her. It has nothing to do with anybody. You just get tired and don't want to be here."

I understood exactly what he was saying. The struggle becomes the predominant reality seeking complete reign. I've been there.

Immediately I thanked him for being willing to struggle to get back to his self; the self who loves his family because he is not PTSD. PTSD wanted to be him, to have his life. It is a separate entity from you. I went straight into prayer: "Satan you are a liar! Give him peace please, Lord! Protect him from harm and danger!" Robert became very quiet and he was ready to get off the phone saying he'd call me back later.

I remember wondering if I should have prayed. Was I being selfish wanting Robert to stick around knowing how tormented his soul was and had been for quite some time? Shouldn't I want him to have eternal peace? What have I done? For sure, I wanted him here with me and his family, but God, if he can't be happy, could I be unfair not letting him go?

Two hours went by and I had not heard from him. I called his cellphone and my call went straight into voicemail. I sat at my desk at work going on like all was well, still feeling strangely fearful, so I called Marcus. We decided it was time to find him, but when he drove to

Robert's home, he was not there. Finally, the Akron Police Department called me and let me know where he was. He had gone to get himself some help at the Veterans Outpatient Clinic. He didn't answer his phone because he did not have access to it. Once a soldier reports they are possibly ending his or her life, security measures are implemented. Not knowing for over two hours where my son was set in motion my need to further understand PTSD beyond my own PTSD diagnosis.

CHAPTER 10
DAILY STRUGGLES WITH PTSD

I understood Robert's impatience with simple things because, behind the scenes, I was battling my own impatience diligently. In reading Morris' book, there were moments tears filled my eyes because it seemed he was talking about me. For instance, he shared an experience where he had gotten so upset with his cell phone, he pretty much cursed at it and butchered it with a knife. It reminded me of times when I'd been alone and cursed my keys or the locks on the door to my home like they were alive just because I had no patience in finding the right key to unlock the door, then felt ashamed once I figure it all out.

If it was not keys, then it could be the simplest of things like realizing I left a sock upstairs after going downstairs to the laundry room, to leaving my cell phone in the car after undressing for bed. I've had a lot of private moments of cursing, none I am proud of, but it seemed to reset my ability to be patient in my daily activities with people. It's like you must constantly monitor yourself to make sure you do not offend innocent people or wreak havoc on normal and wonderful settings. You just do not have time or patience for meaningless gatherings.

I know illogical human behavior can trigger an outburst of reaction because people with PTSD know it is such a waste of time. You just can't fathom how people spend their time and energy in foolish and meaningless situations. Life is too short to induce and participate in unpaid, dramatically induced moments. My goal each day is to come back home. It's like living two different lives; one saving the world from your worst self while the other is being free to just be when you are alone.

Time is a very peculiar phenomenon for PTSD sufferers. I've learned soldiers get trapped into time frames of active trauma experiences. At times, the moments are so real, they lose touch with current realities. Recently I was watching a movie, "Falcon Rising;" the star of the movie, Michael Jai White, was an ex-marine with PTSD. He was a very strong and well-disciplined man skilled in the Martial Arts. Watching him facing life with the disorder was very interesting because, though he moved quickly, he could freeze his reactions to certain situations that could have a horrific outcome. His name was John "Falcon" Chapman in the movie. Falcon had a very powerful presence, yet he could be extremely logical and resourceful. He was on meds for the disorder and carried them around in his pocket. Obviously, it was very clear he did not fear death. It was this key characteristic that allowed him to make perfect decisions to defend himself and others.

Watching Falcon battle with PTSD behind closed doors yet being able to be a practically perfect man when he ventured out into the world was something to respect in great measure. This is how it is done for people with PTSD; we work at finding the best way to do everything we do. This is how we use our time and energy. This gives us rewarding glimpses of indescribable peace.

Because of the moments of being conscious of past traumatic experiences or even lesser experiences brought on by stress, the mind tends to lack the ability to perfectly place experiences in the correct time warp. Emotions pushed to their limits can overtax the mind's ability to keep up with the imbalance of processing overwhelming experiences. The experience is somewhat like when we are using our computers; if we type too fast or search too fast in the search engine, the computer will just freeze as if to say, "Hold up, let me catch up with you."

Our minds can consume every ounce of our experiences, storing information in deep and unending places within our being. So much of the information that is stored is visual lacking words to give us detailed understanding of it. The experiences are not dead; they are packed away and manifest the realities of it in endless ways and during the strangest of times.

Some experiences recalled are referred to as flashbacks, daydreams, nightmares, heartache, illness, and mental disturbances. It is with the mental disturbances that we have come to give many names and branch them out in many categories, such as schizophrenia, depression, anxiety, bipolar, etc. Some effects of the overload of traumatic emotional distribution simply go into forms of amnesia. So much happens to us when stress and trauma attacks our being. There is no way to measure the damages until they manifest, and even then, it is not accurate because the aftermath is so multi-dimensional introducing us to realms of life most people do not want to acknowledge or simply just can't learn the language of it.

I remember realizing how strange my memory was. I saw myself waking up to begin my rituals to start my day and it dawned on me just how new everything seemed. I've awakened feeling extra clean like I just had a fresh shower.

There are pure and beautiful moments of realizing the sweetness of gratitude and peace. Just like the traumatic recalls, we do have ecstatic moments seeming not to be of this world. We carry so many vibrational feelings and emotions, some we can catch and identify them; others get away from us before we understand their message or interpretation of what they consisted of. There is a lot of fleeting thoughts going on inside our minds. Then there are stagnant moments where we go into trances. Some we like and do not fear.

For sure, though we are strong, we are fragile; but we can't let our fragility keep us from growing. We must be willing to do whatever it takes to be free and happy.

Our greatest priority must be to constantly grow our conscious to see who we are. We do this by self-observation. PTSD forces us to deal with the inner and outer world. Our imbalance occurs because we are so busy externally giving our life energy to what we see and neglect the world within.

After war soldiers tend to strive to stay away from within because at times it is such a dark, cold and lonely place. I was talking with a dear friend once whose husband had fought in the Vietnam War. He shared with her that he would have constant nightmares, one, over and over tormenting him. One night he had enough of the torture and took authority and told the images, "You are not real, and you cannot control me anymore!" The dream never came back. He literally rewrote the script.

I have a lot of respect for this man. Though the reality was in his mind, he handled it as though it was in his physical world. The power came when he looked at it for what it was: an image surviving because it was not acknowledged for what it was; a delusion locked in like a photograph by emotional undealt with ties. It just isn't normal to be in a warzone no matter how we justified it.

I remember one night I had made myself a comfortable pallet on the floor. I was having the best sleep when suddenly, I was dreaming a dog was trying to attack me. I commenced to kicking the dog as hard as I could. The next thing I knew, my foot was throbbing in agony from the swift kick to my hardwood dresser. I had fractured one of my toes! The pain was not in my head; it was in my foot.

It appeared my dream images were real enough to project a physical reaction in my physical world. How close are our inner and outer worlds? We exist in a world of imaging which manifests through vibrations. Watching images on our televisions can appear so real at times or have sounds making us think it is happening right there in our space. We have a great responsibility of making sure we distinguish what is or is not real.

CHAPTER 11
THE TRUTH WILL SET YOU FREE: THE CATALYST OF PTSD

PTSD is a direct result of our not accepting reality. The most important word in Post-Traumatic Stress Disorder is STRESS. Remove all the other words to it and you have out of control priorities – this is stress. Humanity has allowed money to control our choices. Who controls the distribution of money? Often, the source is those who declare war. They are the ones who will not become candidates of PTSD. Some soldiers have a quiet anger about this truth and never discuss it with anyone because it can open a can of worms when trying to heal from the disorder. It is another one of those justified anger issues that eventually must be let go to get to our best state of being.

One evening I caught the tail end of a documentary where a veteran from the Vietnam War was diagnosed with PTSD.

He shared his daily suffering with us. Just about every night, he had one repeated flashback and it was him killing an unarmed Viennese man who begged for his life. The man begged that he let him live because he had a son, please I am a father! Ignoring his plea, the soldier killed him. Not only did he kill him, but he loaded his dead body with several bullets.

It was then I realized PTSD can have a hidden catalyst keeping it alive in their minds. For this veteran, he was imprisoned in his own guilt. He doesn't know why he acted so barbaric and heartless. This soldier was angry with the man that killed an unarmed man who was a father. Subconsciously, he was punishing himself for what he viewed as a senseless murder. The warzone was not enough justification for the act. Anger locked him into PTSD. Forgiving himself is the only thing that will unlock it.

Once his therapist could make him see the man carrying the rifle was in war mode, a place where the heart did not have a job, he was on automatic pilot. It was not his call to be anything else. Finally, he could release the anger and live a productive life. I was so thankful to see him smile and eventually chuckle. Unjustified anger and self-anger controls our minds causing us to be unhappy and unhealthy. We must remember that many life experiences have glitches in them like accidents; we don't remember the person we were while it was initially activated. Almost like stepping into a twilight zone and then returning wondering what happened. A lot of experiences are out of our hands, and no matter how undesirable they are, they are going to happen. But know that you survived for a better reason than why it happened to you.

Humanity must approach life in a more humane way instead of the constant need to take, stop and destroy the life of another. We are all affected by a system of unjust power. How do we justify a structure that pays entertainers more money than it pays a soldier, fireman, doctor, teacher, police officer, etc.? This perplexing fact is ignored because we don't understand the systems controlling the world. We just know something is wrong with this picture. We go on like it is not happening. Yet we live with the repercussions of this truth. We live in a world filled with angry people who are angered for various reasons and many people are acting out their anger in forms like road rage, murder, rape, suicide, snapped experiences, etc.

Anger and stress go hand-in-hand and they are sources that grow and multiply when ignored of their hold on our lives. The reality of living in an unjust world takes a toll on the human soul at times allowing the victimizing spirit to slip in. This in turn reduces us to be a desperate presence instead of a serene one. Our soldiers diagnosed with PTSD are bringing to light the impact that ignoring anger and stress is creating a world of walking time bombs. We must individually begin to do things differently. The first thing is to acknowledge we cannot control unjust choices of others. Know the role of stress and anger is to kill and destroy us. Our greatest challenge is to exhale and drop it. Stop where you are, feel the tension of it, let it go constantly. When we do this, our better self takes control allowing us to be godlike. This allows us the ability to be free from worldly conditions that attempt to weather our souls.

The way back to balancing our lives is to individually stop allowing external powers to dictate what is best for us. These sources are driven by accumulating money, not freedom. If we really want to get a grip on Post-Traumatic Stress Disorder, we must understand who and what we are. We are so much more than what meets the eye. We are vast and filled with God's energy that is always permeating vibrations of images waiting for us to choose what will be our realities. The Bible tells us to watch as well as pray. It is a 24/7 job.

How often have we heard what is priceless and most important money can't buy? Yet we allow ourselves to be swept away by worldly systems demanding us to get, get, get, and get. Our society controls us because we do not make having a stress-free life a priority. The old saying, "Too blessed to be stressed," is an excellent saying, but I do not believe most people live it mainly because stress is something no one owns. We would rather let it kill us than to admit it owns us.

We exist in a stress-saturated world, whether it is permeating from us or others, we all get contaminated with it. We become our own antidote when we step out of the trenches and create a growing conscious of self-awareness. As an individual, you must acknowledge your entire self inwardly and outwardly. Work at simplifying your life. What do you really need? What do you really want? Is it worth your life to have it?

We would not have war if each person on the planet knew who and what he or she is. We are individuals with unique experiences and memories. We must love who and what we have become because this is who we are. Jesus accepted who He was and maximized His presence in the world. He is the most famous oddball known to man, yet the most powerful among others who have mastered their roles in life. We cannot afford to go against ourselves because when it is all said and done, we are still who we are. The joy of it is learning to use every experience and element that makes us who we are to have a better and peaceful presence.

Stress pushes us around in so many ways. Oftentimes we are the stress maker because we do not feel we are, nor do enough, to deserve peace. No matter where we are, no one there knows exactly what we are thinking and vice versa. The space for us to survive and have heaven on earth is home. We must make sure it accommodates us to the fullest degree of peace as possible.

When the home is not our heaven on earth, we run the risk of losing our survival base against stress. I am a firm believer to be absent from the body is to be engulfed with all your emotional familiarities. Where we will be placed in heaven will depend on the already existing vibrations of peace we have already created for ourselves while living. This can also apply to positions in hell as well. The moment we walk out the door of our homes, the world of stress takes our hand. If we are geared up with self-love and peace, we can return home and bathe in the welcoming heavenly vibrations we personally created for ourselves. One of our greatest jobs is creating heaven on earth and this can only be done when we consciously realize we are perfect just as we are simply because there is no other existence in the Universe like us.

How did we get so perfect? Our experiences molded us moment by moment from the womb to who we are today. Post-Traumatic Stress Disorder is a wakeup call to know and accept who we are. PTSD has many levels and depths. It can be mild or exceptionally extreme. This is so, no doubt, but we should find a way to diffuse it one step of awareness at a time. For sure love helps. Give it and be receptive of it.

I am always reminded: Yes, yes, yes, I hurt, but this is not all that I am. Life does not care how I feel. What am I going to do?

PART III:

THE GIFT OF FREEDOM

FIRST STEP TO FREEDOM:
BE ENCOURAGED…
A NEW DAY IS HERE!

Hello everybody! I love you!

"Maybe the journey isn't so much about becoming anything. Maybe it's unbecoming everything that isn't you, so you can be who you were meant to be in the first place." Unknown

I shared my life's journey because I wanted you to know that oftentimes, when people go through traumatic experiences in life, we tend to be controlled by one major question: "Who would I have been if this had not happened to me?" This question has stalked me my entire life. It seemed I was having so many victimizing experiences I lost who I was. Not only did I lose who I was, I never really knew who I was from the beginning. But I've learned something along the way and I want to share this with my veterans of war who experienced PTSD.

Know me, and many others, have a heart for you and an invisible bond exist between us all. It is okay, you will never be the same, we know this; but if you think about it, we are never the same ever. Looking at life, all roads point to a journey. We are just passing through here. From the time we were born, we have been becoming. When you spend enough time with children, you begin to see the only thing that is a baby is their bodies; deep within their eyes you see souls on the move.

We suffer because life is very addictive. We get comfortable with familiarity. The moment it changes we experience withdrawal. The effects of withdrawal are very unwanted and painful; it is withdrawal, not who we are. Eventually we must accept change. In time, we get back on the road of our journey. It would be less painful if we stop letting external sources constantly feed us what they want us to think we need to be happy. Avoid people and sources that are negative. Find your own kind. Trust yourself and God. Always remember, no matter what is going on in the world, God is in and with you. Each one of us are individuals empowered to be great children of God simply because there is only one of us on the entire planet. Do not let justified anger own you. It has no rights. It cannot exist without you.

When you see your fellow man, remember he or she may or may not have been to war, but they have experienced pain and injustice. They may not have learned your deep level of gratitude and appreciation for the simplistic things in life, but they are human and need to be loved and understood also. Don't judge or punish them for your choices. We are all fragile.

We must be conscious of what we focus on. What we give our attention to owns us in that moment. When it does not feel right, shift gears, choose to be love. And what is love? Peace to our life and the lives of others. Trauma forces change; stress forces you to do something. Choose wisely. Save yourself. Only you can confirm your value.

For me each day is a brand-new day. I awake to learn where I am.

"There's a lot of stress out there, and to handle it, you just need to believe in yourself; always go back to the person that you know you are, and don't let anybody tell you any different, because everyone's special and everyone's awesome."

~ McKayla Maroney

CHAPTER 12
FIRST STEP TO FREEDOM:
BE WILLING TO LEARN

"When the student is ready, the teacher will appear."
Zen Proverb

The fact that you have reached this page confirms you are ready for the ultimate truth that will set you free: You are indeed the Inevitable You who wants to receive and live the best life possible.

You are about to enter the classroom of PTSD to Freedom. Your instructor, William Sumner is a veteran of the United States Army and he will be sharing with you his experience, expertise and wisdom that will provide life-changing tools that release the chains attached to PTSD.

Keep in mind, this is not your ordinary class because this class connects more to the subconscious mind than it does to the conscious mind. It may appear at times that you are not fully getting the concepts based on your conscious intake. Do not be discouraged, hang in there because before you reach the end of this class, you will experience a phenomenal shift in conscious that will change your life forever for the better. Get excited, you are going to love it! And remember, truth always transforms.

William Sumner will be re-introducing tools we are already using but are not maximizing because we simply are not aware we are using them because we live life on autopilot which you will begin to see as he reveals the power of our mind and emotions.

He is an advocate of waking people up to their Inevitable Selves. We are great survivors of traumatic experiences in our lives making us quite resilient time and time again, William does not want us to be just resilient; he wants us to have healthy responses to life's traumatic experiences by having our inner resources solidified with facts and beliefs to the highest power possible which will create a foundation of automatic choices towards our greatest good. Not that we will be zombies or robots unable to feel, we would be human beings facing life with an understanding that we do not have to be drowned and controlled by our emotions to a point of losing best; I guess you could say we will be more like resilience with grace. Let's begin.

CHAPTER 13
TRUST IN PTSD TO PTSG: INTRODUCTION

Hello! My name is William Sumner. I am so excited to serve and share tools that will improve every area of your life. As a veteran of the United States Army, I found after serving my term I was still eager to serve people on the highest level possible. Experiences taught me that no matter what we experience, the mind is our greatest tool to success.

I came up with "The Inevitable You ® Coaching System" designed to help people grow, change, transform and heal their lives in ways that they never considered possible.

It is tools-based and very intentional, it is not "rah-rah" motivation. Everyone has an "operating system" that solves problems, dictates dreams, creates appropriate caution and risk management, chooses actions to take or don't take, etc. It is this "mental software" that creates reality, and when you change the programs contained within it, everything else changes.

Doing anything to improve your success and happiness has value, however, the greatest value is in designing and installing a complete new set of "mental software".

It is a coaching system that is setup to help you accelerate at unprecedented levels, should you choose to use it to its fullest extent. And, it is easily teachable to others. "The Inevitable You ® Coaching System" is the foundation that gets you from PTSD to PTSG.

As I was developing this program, I realized my fellow comrades responded well to the tools I offered when they came to me for assistance as they battled with PTSD. In fact, I found that people who had faced traumatic experiences from rape, sexual abuse, death, illness, divorce, natural disaster, you name it, they gained a better or new walk in life once they realized they are the ones who always made that possible.

When you have a large vision of making a difference in the world and your ideals and execution of bringing it to past are not quite of the norm or orthodox, it is a kind of a lonely but a very acceptable journey. Fortunate for me that one day someone I hold in high esteem revealed his take on PTSD to PTSG. It was a moment of humbleness and excitement for me especially because I did not know this amazing article existed. It was an article in the **Military 1** online magazine featuring Retired Marine General Jim Mattis, one of the most beloved and feared military leaders in modern history. He was sharing his true views on Post-Traumatic Stress Disorder before a group of veterans and how it is handled by professionals.

I grew more and more ecstatic as I read the entire article because he and I were on the same page in how we viewed the PTSD labelling our soldiers receive when they return home from war.

General Mattis admits the approach with assisting our veterans with PTSD had to change if we wanted our soldiers to beat the diagnosis. The best solution for healing that he came up with was

PTSG, Post-Traumatic Stress Grow. He fully understood how labels bound people to a limited state of being. Like me, he insists the label of Post-Traumatic Stress Disorder is too limiting and damaging for our veterans. And, it is important that we let our veterans know they are not damaged goods limited to a victimized life. Instead, our veterans are amazing people who do not need to be identified as victims.

And, our veterans do not have to assume professionals have all the answers to the best way to heal soldiers diagnosed with PTSD. However, it is important to note, when we proceed to remove the labeled diagnosis of PTSD to PTSG, anyone diagnosed with Post-Traumatic Stress Disorder must realize it is up to them to remove and replace the labels themselves if they want to be healed.

I am confident, I have the tools to assist our soldiers in removing the PTSD label. It is with great honor and respect that I hand you the keys to freedom.

CHAPTER 14
PREPARATION FOR REMOVING: THE PTSD LABEL

Being that everything begins within the mind, I want you to take a deep breath and relax while I take you through the journey of the roles the conscious and unconscious minds have on our choices. Once you see our responses and actions in life are influenced on automatic pilot, you will know, you can program that pilot to have the best responses and choices possible for positive and productive life experiences. I want to begin with what is known as the software of our minds whether we acknowledge it or not, Neuro-Linguistic Programming, or NLP is managing our life's roadmap to power.

NLP provides simple ways in which we can change the way we think, view past events, and how we approach life. It is our automatic recall system where we unknowingly draw from to respond to the life's experiences we encounter daily.

We are going to learn how to take control of our mind. NLP is more about controlling what is happening on the inside of us than trying to control what is happening outside of us. NLP, Neuro-Linguistic Programming is a tool we do not hear about daily, yet it has so much to offer us. It is very controversial in its ability to bring about healthy changes in thought and behavior. Maybe it is somewhat a secret because it offers people an opportunity to be independent and at times to not need medications to heal their psychological diagnosis. I personally have found NLP to be an excellent choice to freedom.

I realize that Neuro-Linguistic Programming sounds kind of far out there, but it really isn't. It is our way of navigating through life from inside out. NLP is simple, but massively, massively effective, and powerful for shifting how we think, feel, focus, believe, change, and create our actions and behavior.

First thing to understand about Neuro-Linguistic Programming is that we have two sources of communication: We repeatedly speak and think our sentences. Both sources are powerful in determining outcome.

Why do you believe one individual sentence, and let's say it's a positive one, meaning you can, you are, or believe another sentence, you cannot, you never will? Why is one sentence true versus another one? The fact of the matter is they're only true because you continue to say them repeatedly. Now, the science is what you say, and this is the linguistics of it, and because you're thinking, which is only silent verbal communication to yourself. In Linguistic, what you say and think, and the words have meanings and when you emotionalize them it solidifies the words to be true.

This strongly implies to anyone diagnosed and accepting the PTSD label. Because you have raw, real emotions attached to it and no one has explained to you in a comprehensible way that you control the emotions, you accept this as truth that you have Post-Traumatic Stress Disorder and you don't expect to be anything different. This is your reality and in some cases your need to survive.

You became instantly tied to the words of the doctor because your emotions were stimulated, raised so high and charged with negative energy that PTSD became somewhat a life sentence of torture. If someone tried to tell you no, don't buy into that PTSD label, you don't hear them because you have yet to realize what part you play in keeping it real.

This is a fundamental problem because you don't know how to change your belief. And, you don't realize what you are believing. You just know what you were told is what it is and your feelings during and after diagnosis made it real in your subconscious.

It never enters your mind to change or question what is true here. Yet you are constantly exercising your power of deciding what IS truth. This is where NLP comes in at, changing your programmed database. You can wipe out the moment of impact when your emotions tied to the words of the doctor and replace it with something far more powerful and positive.

For instance, I was approached by a veteran during one of my seminars and he said, "Here's my trigger," he said, "I'm in college and it just bugs the crap out of me. I don't know why, I've talked to my therapist, I mean, it is obvious why is it sounds like a gunshot when they slam their books down. But when kids come in and they throw their books on their desks and they don't even really care that they're free to be there, that my buddies died, I should've died, and I carry guilt, it torments me."

I realized instantly he's in classic PTSD mode, so I said, "Well, wait a second. If the sounds of books hitting, gives you this horrible memory triggering a popping of gunfire, what does a big flag over a cemetery do on a windy day, isn't it popping in the breeze too?"

What if you said the books were freedom, the books popping sound were a flag? You get to know that you're okay. You get to know that your buddies did not die in vain. They are providing this freedom. Can you reframe it? Can you emotionalize these trigger events? And then that once you get good reframing for this, we just must go through all the trigger events and reprogram, program the Neuro-Linguistic Program to make this a positive, powerful event. So, we're going to reframe. We're going to take the trauma and we're going to turn it into your greatest strength, your greatest positive.

NLP empowered him to see and respond to things differently. Not only that, it allowed him to see his world map blueprint and redirect its programed directions to a better state of being. He saw his triggers were created from habitual intensity of an event causing his emotions to solidify it as a true response to life. He didn't have to think about it, the feelings and thoughts about it was engraved in his subconscious with no judgment. This soldier saw the dynamics of creating truth and changed it to move forward with freedom from the unwanted response brought on by previously unintentional creation. He literally interrupted the autopilot and became the pilot of his truths. Awesome!

Let me share another example of real life change. This woman stood up in one of my seminars once and she said, "You know, I was married to a very, very rich husband. He has a very, very rich family and we have a 13-year-old daughter. I fought, fought, fought, and I fought in court, they outspent me, they out pushed me, they out punished me. I was lied to. I have lost my daughter. There is no way you can make that a better than we are or a positive moment."

And I said, "Yeah, I get that you're in a lot of pain." You know, so sometimes in the laws of life, you know, get it now or die, quit, the Law of Attraction, or the I create my reality laws, some of the new age stuff, I realized that bad things happen, bad things happen sometimes to good people. So, we can't undo that but here's where we can begin to make better than we are real. I said, "First of all, I want you to create something I like to call a memory box. And here's what I'm going to guarantee you, even if it's six years from now that your daughter's emancipated. She's 19. She wants to come looking for you. She's mad at you because you gave up. The family lied about you. In this memory box, every day, if not every day, nearly every day, you're at Chipotle's, put a menu in there, write a note on it.

"You know, honey, I was at Chipotle's. I was thinking the last time we had guacamole and chips and how much you love them. I'm thinking of you." Put a date on it. Take a photograph of a favorite place. "I'm thinking of you." You see something come on the TV, snap a picture on your smartphone, print it. You can put daily memories into this memory box. Six years from now it's probably going to be five memory boxes full and when she comes hunting for you, you're going to say to her, "Look honey, I want to show you something. I have five boxes that I want you to look at and look through, and I want you to know six years ago I spent every dime fighting for you."

What did I do? I gave her an opportunity to reprogram her heart-breaking experience of losing her daughter by empowering her to do something that she had the power to do and that is to create memories that no one could take from her.

On autopilot, the emotional tie of experiencing seeing her husband take her daughter wore her down inside leaving her to not have hope. She didn't even have to think about it. It was solidified in her mind because of intense and habitual emotions responding to her rich husband's determination to win.

Once she saw something beautiful and attainable, the autopilot was reprogramed ending her state of hopelessness. Boy, I love this!

CHAPTER 15
THE BRAIN IS THE HARD DRIVE FOR THE MIND

I am sure you are beginning to see Neuro-Linguistic Programming is a pattern of sentences, and words, and a pattern of thoughts that can convey reality at a habitual level. So, when you think about what is real, it's the neurons and this thing I call software, meaning you have this little two-and-a-half-pound hard drive that's between your ears. Instead of being silicon, plastic, and electricity, it's fat, water, and electricity. That is the hard drive, and then you have an unseen operating system with a series of equations that's the programming part, because you habitually say the same pattern of words, you unknowingly believe them to be true. Oftentimes it begins when you say, "I am," or "I am not."

In the case of PTSD, instead of habitually engraving the truth, we can also substitute the engraving with intense. So, a one-time intense can be your first responder like an IED in the Middle East, or a woman being traumatized in an attack. Intensity will do the same brain chemistry as habitual. The great news about that is if intense is real programing, guess what? You can override it with new habitual sentences, it will change the hard drive's chemistry.

Just think about it, you now have a new basis to ponder possibilities. And the memories that you worry about, that trauma… any sentences you put together and this is also includes good memories like becoming captain of the football team, that's when I got a straight A report card, that's when I experienced my trauma, acute or chronic, it doesn't matter, all of it is just a bundle of neurons running a pattern in a way that was either fused habitually or fused with intensity. We can undo what we don't want and intensify what we do want. It all begins the moment we realize we have a choice.

Your thoughts, feelings, and emotions are not things that are, or that you have, but things that you do. They are your responses to life. Their causes can often be very complicated, involving, for instance, comments or beliefs from your parents or teachers, or events that you have experienced.

NLP shows you how you can take control of these beliefs and influences. Using mind techniques such as visualization and affirmations, can change the way that you think and feel about past events, fears and even phobias.

One important awareness you must become clear about is what do you believe because what you believe is very powerful.

If you believe you are sick and might die, you probably will. On the flip side though if a healer came to town and tells you to drink this and live a long life you probably will live a long and healthy life. It just depends on the emotional execution of receiving the words you hear.

No matter who or when someone told you something, your belief in it determines if you will or will not do or be in a positive or negative state. So, one of the first things you must do is take time out to see and know what controls your choices. Recognize the limiting beliefs. Focus in on each one of them and question their validity and contributions to your life. If you do not like it, change the language. Tell yourself, I am more than that and from this day forward, I am acting differently because I believe differently.

When you have this type of awareness, stress takes on a different meaning. Responses to daily life's moment by moment events are more in balance of what you prefer. Anxiety lessens, and peace of mind increases.

We are getting closer to removing the PTSD label. Our next tool is putting stress where it belongs, in a very positive place.

CHAPTER 16
STRESS PERSPECTIVES

I want to begin by defining stress from the positive perspective because daily we constantly hear about the downside of stress which does exist, but we are on the road of getting beyond that.

When you think about stress, you think about people living the hustle and bustle of life. We must pay the bills, take care of children, our aging parents, get that A on a test, be accepted by our friends and peers, etc. Yes, this is stress, but stress must be conceived on another level for us to get to freedom.

How often have we shared the positive purposes of stress? Almost never, right?

Very seldom do people talk about stress with excitement. But, without stress, we do not heal and grow. The missing link to the positive side of stress is found in eustress which is: positive stress having a beneficial effect on our health, motivation, performance, and emotional well-being.

For instance, you're in the gym nearing the home stretch of completing your workout you're doing that last curl in the gym, the 10th rep and you're using good form, what's literally happening in the muscle belly is experiencing violent cellular death. Cells are bursting under the stress of that last rep. And the wisdom of your body is saying, "Hey, I need to make those daughter cells, a little bigger, a little stronger." So that's how you build your bicep, with eustress.

The flipside to eustress comes when we do not already have the foundation to receive the reps to grow the muscles due to poor nutrition, lack of sleep, poor form, you haven't made it to the gym in a while, you're lifting too hard and you have a rupture of the muscle cells, you tear your bicep, which causes distress which takes us from positive stress to toxic stress.

Toxic stress reveals something happened to weaken the base because it was not prepared for eustress. But listen to me clearly: this does not mean healing will not occur and that growth will not happen. In fact, when we heal toxic stress, the muscle cells are going to be stronger. The body will make sure that ruptured bicep comes back stronger from the tear. It's just that the rehab is going to take a little bit longer.

Toxic stress does not have the last say so nor does trauma. One thing I have learned without a doubt healing and growth occurs in the most horrific life situations. Be it a veteran, civilian, first responder, cop, fireman, teachers in distressful school environments after shootings, anybody who has experienced distress, who knows they were broken, ruptured and suffering inside who went through rehab have admitted experiencing surreal strength through it all.

Though the tools offered may not heal everyone who has suffered with trauma back to perfect, the truth is many are going to be healed back better than they were. Just like the bicep is stronger for having undergone violent cellular death, it became stronger. If we do the work, most are going to be stronger than they were before Post-Traumatic Stress Disorder. So, keep in mind we have eustress which is positive stress and we have toxic stress that reveals we are not prepared for impact.

Remember, regardless to what we experience in life, we have a choice to how we program our world map.

CHAPTER 17
THE IMPACT OF LABELLING

Studies have proven time and time again that it's the power of labels that's creating the basis for what we believe. The sad thing about labelling is that usually the labeler nor the one being labeled realize it is occurring. The labeler is someone you trust and value their perspective of you. For example, a common one is a teacher's impact on a student.

The teacher, nor the students, know that they've been mislabeled from bright kids to troublemakers. So, they take a bright class and run a six-week test, they label them as troublemakers and take troublemakers and label them as bright kids. Not only do the kids feel different, the teachers treated them differently and the actual test scores changed significantly on the lower and higher end of scores all based on the power of labels.

Placebo testing is well known and often have anywhere from 20% to 40% success in their experiment. If people don't know they are taking placebos but was just told they were, the outcome is even higher, often, more than 40% because they believe what they were told. Noceboes are just the opposite, you get bad news that's not true, but if you believe it, it could be the beginning of the end.

One of my most powerful examples on the nocebo effect took place in the late '80s when AIDS was scaring the crap out of everybody. Back in the day a movie was made. Ryan White was this little 14-year-old kid that had AIDS from his mother from a blood transfusion. Modern technology was nothing like it is today in the medical field so when blood tests were done, they made the testing very open because they wanted to catch a lot of samples, which meant they would have a lot of false positives. Whether the patients had AIDS or not, they were told they had it. So, about 10 years later when they went back in and retested the blood they collected, not only did they go, "Oh hey, here's thousands of false positives, let's go tell them so that they won't have to worry about it any longer. Not only did they find over 90% of them had passed away, when they looked at the cause of death, they died of AIDS because they were told they had it and they strongly believed it. This power of labels is incredibly, incredibly powerful. It all begins by receiving words into our emotional bodies. Our conscious and unconscious minds take it as truth and you live it spontaneously. The good news is that because you are now aware of how this process takes place, input and outcome can be changed. Before we complete this class, I am going to cover with you your ability to associate and dissociate word combinations that threaten your emotional control of choices. But first we must say goodbye to the PTSD label.

CHAPTER 18
GOODBYE PTSD LABEL

We are a step away from removing the PTSD label. But first we must know exactly what it means to say goodbye to Post-Traumatic Stress Disorder and hello to Post-Traumatic Stress Growth.

We have already learned eustress creates a field for growth. We learned the physical process to how stress leads to growth. Now let's learn the psychological process to stress growth.

I want to emphasize that the body and mind's rehab ability to make you stronger after traumatic experiences are real and my tools of success are very real also. How you are spoken to when you are diagnosed with PTSD is crucial to the outcome of your healing process. For instance, if I was skiing in Vail, during winter time and had a horrible break and had to go into the emergency room and the attending doctor said, "Oh, my God. That is one of the worst breaks I've ever seen. But I have good news, I'm a bad ass, I can fix that. The better news is you're going to walk. But I have bad news, 90% of my patients will limp with that kind of break."

When we studied this doctor's patients, 90% of them limp. Now, if it's a parallel universe day and it's the same leg break only this time it's a different doctor that walks in and she says, "Oh, my God. That's one of the worst I've seen. But I have good news, I'm a bad ass, I can fix it. Better news is you can walk, and the great news, and it is great, but I have to tell you, the rehab is very, very arduous, but 90% of my patients walk fine." When we study her patients, they walk fine. Now, the reason why this is massively important to you, and anyone curious about how Post-Traumatic Stress Growth works, it's these two points. How someone tells you how you are doing can make or break you.

When people limp into my office to work with me and I ask them, "What happened to you?" They never say, "Oh, you know what? I got screwed on a parallel universe day. I got the wrong labeling doctor and I believed the wrong label." They tell me about the accident, how awful it was, how they had one of the best surgeons in the Valley work on it and my leg will never be as good as it was before the accident.

They believe the label they've been given.

Now, the more important piece of this is when your body looks at it. This is critical. I asked the question, when your body looks at this and does its thing, immune system activation, healing activation, neural chemistry working in the autonomic nervous system to heal you, do you believe that the body attempts to return you 100% good as new? Yeah, it does, but it's not good as new. It's broken. And the answer is better than this. I've already told you, any time something breaks in the body, it makes it better than new because new was not good enough.

You just have to know in rehab to take advantage of the power labels have, "What happened to me? I did have the stress. It's post-trauma. How am I better than new?" You are better than new because the body uses the trauma to rebuild.

Many of you are suffering, going through therapy and taking medications under the care of professionals who really care about you. None of them would be considered evil or stupid. They are just practicing an older science, and this science doesn't see you as Post-Traumatic Stress Growth. It sees you as Post-Traumatic Stress Disorder. There's something wrong with you now. They do not see you as better than new. But you will see it and live it for the rest of your life because your understanding of knowing why you accepted the label is becoming clearer.

You are now free to move from PTSD to PTSG because you know you grow through post-traumatic stress response. You do not become less, you become much more. Words have been implanted into your hard drive throughout this course to begin the journey of endless control over your life and freedom. The work has already started, and you will continue to become more conscious of your positive responses in daily life experiences and situations.

Before you go, I want to share an exercise with you that you can share with anybody. This is a very active and a great visual that reveals how we can change our response and perspective of events.

"I want you to choose a time where you had a specific one-person conflict. I want the emotion involved during that time to be about 6 or 7 from a scale of 1 thru 10. This makes the memory to be a medium-plus.

The first thing I want you to do is see what you saw then hear what you heard now I want you to feel with the same intensity.

I want your memory to be as vivid as possible so much, so you see skin pores in their face. See all the intrinsic signs of anger this person spewed towards you.

Now I want you to see you and this person on the big movie screen. Next, I want you to turn the sound up, vibrating sound with the bass. At this point the anger scale should be nearing 10 because the bass sound intensifies the experience.

Now, I want you to release the memory, exhale and clear the screen. Excellent! This memory is in your subconscious and conscious memory. It is never dead. Triggers are attached to it effecting your life at any time, but I want to take that same memory and begin again with the same commands we previously started with the first exercise, but we will move through the process a little quicker. See what you saw then, hear what you heard now feel what you felt. This time I want you to put the person who angered you in a little black and white kitchen TV that is sitting in a corner. This time no bass to turn up you can barely hear them talking even though the person is just as mad and angry as they were in the first recall. In fact, you can barely see them because the little black and white TV can reveal only so much intensity.

While that person is in that little box, I want you to take the person and pick your favorite cartoon character, and I always use Bugs Bunny, put Bugs Bunny ears on them and use Bugs Bunny's voice. Now they're over there, they are just as mad except now they're talking in, 'Hey, Doc,' this is Bugs Bunny's voice. See, you now have control of this memory. It is way less intense.

The last thing that I do, and you can do it too is I put it on a long extension cord because when I did it in my early days, people would say, "Well, the TV can't work without an extension." Talking about, "Put a really long extension cord on it, take it down your driveway, across the street, and put it in your neighbor's front yard. Now, put a number on it from one through 10."

Two things happen to virtually 90% of people who did this exercise: One – mainly because no one wants a bad memory everybody lowers their memory down to one or two or non-existent, they're chuckling. The second thing, you will never go back to that memory and have it become a six or a seven again. You've changed that memory because you like to take the bad away and feel good. You can control your emotions.

You can also put wanted emotions in your body before they are true by putting them on a big movie screen, big sound and big special effects. Remember, you are the editor of your life. You control the special effects of your life. You are the scriptwriter. You get to pick the habitual senses. You don't have to use senses people have programmed you about PTSD. You can choose PTSG. See PTSD as a step to a better you. PTSG, Post-Traumatic Stress Growth is apparent because you had the psychological muscles to accelerate growth. The proof is in your survival.

In closing, keep in mind Post-Traumatic Stress Growth is not a quick fix to surviving distress from traumatic experiences. It is an opportunity to see things differently.

PTSG is an inner unfolding of seeing and feeling differently as you move forward. It is a removing of the PTSD label as well as any other label limiting your ability to grow out of suffering.

Post-Traumatic Stress Growth gives us an opportunity to say, "hey wait a minute, I have some say so about what this will mean to me, I will decide my label, not you!"

CONCLUSION

First, I want you to know it was such a joy having you in my class. I hope what you have learned will be shared with others. In the days to come, you will be amazed to how your subconscious is already utilizing the truths you have received.

These tools are not just about living the life of PTSD to PTSG. They are in fact great tools that enhances every area of your life. You will begin to find the best way to do everything especially with your time. Things will become clearer as far as what is your moment to moment priorities. You are going to love how stress will become less of an issue when it comes to reacting to life's least to greatest experiences. It is almost like being born again.

To think, it all began with NLP... Neuro-Linguistic Programming.

Before I go, I would like to share a question and answer period of me and a fellow veteran who has incorporated these tools in his life. Keep in mind this is just a surface example of how I interact with other veterans seeking answers to the best way to live with PTSD to PTSG.

Veteran: "Hello?"

Bill: "Yes."

Veteran: "Hey, I'm good, Bill, how are you?"

Bill: "Good. Did you catch my dream answer for you?"

Veteran: "I did, and it was a great answer. I knew Bill and I were veterans, and we talked a lot and I got to thinking about what he had to say about Post-Traumatic Stress Disorder. And me and some of my local Houstonian friends have been talking about Post-Traumatic Stress Growth and how the narrative needs to change and is changing, and convinced Bill to put this webinar together. So, I really appreciate that he's doing this for us. And I hope that we can do it again. But back to the subject, yes…"

Bill: "Thank you."

Veteran: "It's awesome. And so even recently, after 10 years or more removed from combat, I hear friends of mine posting things on social media or telling me directly about sleep problems, dreams, recurring memories. And so, I try to, you know, kind of give them some of these tools, but it's always best to hear it from the expert."

Bill: "Perfect. Thank you, we work to solve a serious problem. And we have a lot of empathy and hurt for vets and first responders and people that suffer. There is real pain here. I am here speaking generally and would like to go more in-depth in the future. I want you to begin by thanking. So, thank the bad dream, give it a lot of gratitude. It is trying to tell you something. Keep listening. Ask for positive dreams. This is very important, ask for the message to be made in a good dream. Realize you can talk to your subconscious. So, when you're busy, fighting your dreams and hating your dreams and not wanting to sleep because the bad dreams are going on, know you have the challenge of opposing the bad dreams by putting positive emotions in your body when you are not dreaming.

"Expect to be excited that you are going to have a great dream tonight because you commanded it and it's going to bring you the message in a good dream. I'm just going to tell you, things will begin to flip. For some people, they flip very quickly. Others take a little time.

"It's amazing how nobody who, even if they go to bed and have a nightmare go, 'Well, it didn't work last night. But it's going to work tonight.' And even the fact that they're excited and anticipating sleep for the first time in 10 years, because maybe for 10 years they hated sleep because it's when the dark night of the soul visits them. And so, now that they legitimately get to participate in beginning tonight, they don't have to feel dread. They just have to feel the habitual sentence and say, 'I'm excited to go to sleep tonight because the message is going to come. I know it's going to come in a positive, happy dream.' And, I may not understand what the message is, but I am sure going to try to find out.

"People have to understand it not just your mind remembering bad shit to torture you. The mind doesn't do that. The mind subconsciously tries to communicate with you. These are neural patterns that are firing in your sleep in a way that should heal you. It would have been better if someone would have told you this was a healing process as opposed to someone wanting to drug you so that you would have dreamless sleep. You may feel better in that moment because you didn't have a nightmare last night, but you also didn't have much REM sleep either. So, thank you, great question. Is there anything else I can do for you, sir?"

Veteran: "Okay, good deal. Yeah, I'm just trying to think of some of the other issues...a lot of the guys, because it's been a while since they were in a combat zone, some of their PTSD or PTSG issues are related to family, marriage, things like that. Some of the retreats that I've been to, this is a recurring thing in that relationships are falling apart. Can you address that?"

Bill: "Well, it's generally the reason why life falls apart post-combat. You know, one, they don't feel normal in the world. They feel different and it's worse than normal, they feel less than normal so when you're feeling less than normal, instead you're experiencing this as pain. So, you are not letting them in. It is not because you don't like or love them, you just do not feel like they understand. Truth is, they don't understand a lot of times, and they're rah, rah, cheerleading, they love you, come on it does not help.

"And two, you don't want them to feel the pain. So, there is this bottling process that takes place, and it's really...you know, my tool for this, dear friend, and you know how I love my tools, this one is called 'the hotel door in a fire.' You know, if you're asleep in a hotel room and the fire alarm goes off, the first thing you do when you wake up is you put your hand on the door. By putting your hand on the door, if it's hot, you don't go there. So, if you are in this bottling process, and now even if they want to talk, you don't feel like talking because you bottled it, guess what the door is? The door is hot. So, you don't go there. So, the cutting off process continues, and there is no hope, there's no future world, you know, short of what they are dealing with? Going to the VA, getting therapy, perhaps they're on meds, perhaps they hate what their meds do to them. So, they're getting their scripts, they're not taking their meds, you know, blah, blah, blah.

"There's no future, that they're taught, that they're going to be free of this. So, this cutting off process, this bottling off process, for very good reasons, turn into breakup and pain as opposed to, in a very short turning, the popping of a book from gunfire to popping of flag meaning freedom.

"I have to tell you, there is so much more to processing this, we can help you, call Brian, we can work with you and you're not going to get months and months of laying on somebody's couch. You're going to look at a very specific memory or memory sequence that's tormenting you, and we're going to reframe it, rehab it for what's the strength, how am I better? We're going to re-emotionalize it. So, if you take the bad memory, you're going to reframe it so that you know that you are better than you are, and then you're going to repurpose and re-emotionalize it.

"And now in that process, you can give your loved ones all the love, joy, and gratitude.

'Tell them something like thank you for being with me as I battle through this reprogramming process, because at the end of the day I'm going to be better, which means we are better.'

"And it's real. It's not bullshit. It's not motivational rah-rah. It's real. So that's very generalized but an idea of how it goes.

"When soldiers return home from war, they are cut off from everybody there's nothing bridging or pulling it back together, and there's no hope that it can be. both sides are experiencing that pain. So be it spouse, child, friends or work, people don't understand.

"I've learned through the Law of Attraction that as human beings, it is our nature to plan and request our desires. I have mentioned to you how powerful the subconscious mind is. I should tell you, I have the deepest gratitude for it. If you don't do anything else, thank your subconscious mind constantly for the work it does for you.

"It works 24/7 processing data the conscious cannot contain. Our dreams are a result of our subconscious trying to process and relay information to us. I thank my subconscious even when my dreams are horrible and are nightmares because it dealt with it while I slept instead of while I was awake. Thank you, thank you, thank you!

"I have to confess, I also put my subconscious to work knowing how busy it is because I need answers to how to do things the best way possible. Anybody who knows me know I give myself three hours from 11:00 pm to 2:00 pm to specifically for commanding my subconscious what I wanted to dream and what I wanted to work on because I'm asking for answers. I'm asking for more awareness. My subconscious is deeper and smarter than I am.

"Commanding your dream structure, to believe that you control your dreams is another excellent tool in changing the software of truths and beliefs. Give it a try. Program your future before you fall asleep. In time, you will see it is well worth it. Let this be a very powerful and positive time for you. Believe greatness can emerge.

"Good sample: I am not wanting bad dreams change to: I want epic dreams. There's an entire uplifting process that we can take sleep and we can take dreams and make it work to our advantage. Your life will improve. It's not time that heals your life. This is very important. I want you to understand this. It's not time that heals it. It's changing the habitual sentence that you make about your dreams that will bring healing."

I know you have absorbed a lot of pertinent information. Don't sweat it, you got this! And, if you would like to ask me questions or just want to elaborate further on anything I have shared, feel free to reach out to me at william@theinevitableyou.com. I will always be your teacher and support.

Please visit my website for more information at:
https://www.theinevitableyou.com.

Take care, it has been a pleasure sharing this information with you!

ABOUT THE AUTHORS

LINDA DIANE WATTLEY

LINDA DIANE WATTLEY is a veteran of the United States Army. She is an advocate for sufferers of PTSD, Post-Traumatic Stress Disorder and for those who have suffered from all forms of victimization to include domestic violence and sexual abuse. Her message is all about getting to the best truths that allows victims to be set free. Linda accomplishes this by sharing her gifts and talents that God gave her. One being an author of several books that lead readers to go deep within themselves to find their own inner strength and voice.

Linda was also a contributing columnist, "THE BEST WILL SHOW THEMSELVES" for over twelve years where she shared truths that stirred hearts and minds of readers in spiritual matters.

Today, she has opened a platform for others to share their truths with the world. Her online television show, THE TRUTH WILL SET YOU FREE by TLBTV and the Liberty Beacon Project has proven to be a powerful beacon of light.

Linda is available for speaking engagements, book signings and interviews. She lives to do God's Will.

WILLIAM SUMNER

WILLIAM SUMNER is a veteran of the United States Army and a graduate of West Point. His service included Infantry, Ranger, and Special Operations at home and abroad. He is an internationally sought-after speaker and was one of the top-rated speakers within the Anthony Robbins organization for six years.

Sumner created The Inevitable You® Coaching System designed to help people grow, change, transform, and heal their lives. It's designed to help you discover and embrace who you are, and what you came here to be. This coaching system works both on the business and personal levels of achieving a greater consciousness of productivity and balance in mind and spirit.

This coaching system also takes the best of the best in personal growth, psychology, and leadership, molds it into a framework you can access, and translates it so that you can apply it to your own life. It's designed to help you discover and embrace who you are, and what you came here to be.

Along with creating this amazing coaching system, William Sumner authored "The Inevitable You: Live Life by Design", a self-help book revealing a tools-based and experiential driven system that will allow you to change and transform anything about you at any time, at any level.

It is a simple and easy-to-read guide created from newer, technology-based sciences blended with many ancient wisdom systems to truly release "old you" programs, patterns, and perceptions! It could very well be the book you have been waiting your whole life to read.

For more information on William and The Inevitable You® Coaching System, please visit website:

https://www.theinevitableyou.com
where you can find more free contents, the *Live Life by Design* book, and various online coaching programs. For more information and a free presentation on how to more effectively overcome PTSD from William, please visit

https://theinevitableyou.com/ptsg

www.ingramcontent.com/pod-product-compliance
Lightning Source LLC
Chambersburg PA
CBHW060802050426
42449CB00008B/1496